W9-ASY-510

Ravenscourt
B·O·O·K·S

RACE TO THE NORTH POLE

By

Sharon Franklin

Columbus, OH • Chicago, IL • Redmond, WA

The **McGraw·Hill** Companies

Photos: Cover, ©Hulton Archive/Getty Images;
19, ©Corbis; **40,** ©Hulton Archive/Getty Images;
49, ©Bettmann/Corbis.

Maps: Paul Montgomery

Page 9 [1]Used by permission of Bowdoin College
Library.

SRAonline.com

 SRA

Send all inquiries to:
SRA/McGraw-Hill
8787 Orion Place
Columbus, OH 43240-4027

Printed in the United States of America.

ISBN 0-07-601599-8

1 2 3 4 5 6 7 8 9 MAL 08 07 06 05 04 03

— Chapter 1—

The Race Is On

Matthew Henson had big dreams. His difficult childhood had taught him to turn each hardship into a challenge and then to overcome each challenge.

When Henson met Robert E. Peary, it was the beginning of a successful partnership. The men shared the same desire to succeed. Their bond was even stronger because they shared a goal. They both wanted to walk where no one had ever gone before. They wanted to reach the top of the world.

Where is the top of the world? It is the North Pole—a dot on a map, an invisible point in the Arctic Circle. There is no land at the North Pole, only ice moving over the ocean. It's a lonely, rugged place where winds whip across icy peaks.

Half of each year the North Pole is covered in darkness. In spring the sun returns, filling the sky for months with endless daylight. This is called *the midnight sun.*

Imagine the stories that could be told about such a place! But who would tell them? Only animals such as walrus, whales, polar bears, reindeer, and seals live within the Arctic Circle.

Many explorers have tried to reach the North Pole. Each dreamed of being the first person to stand there. Many people died trying to get to the Pole. Their bodies lie frozen in their sunken ships—proof of adventures gone wrong. Those who survived returned with chilling tales of failure. They told of winds that reached 60 degrees below zero—winds that turned their skin black with ice.

Survivors reported seeing bodies frozen solid on the sides of ice peaks. They told of snow so white that it blinded those who dared to look too long. They talked of shifting sheets of ice called *floes* that could crush large ships like small bugs. If all this were not enough, they said the magnetic pull of the North Pole caused compasses to go crazy. This caused explorers to get lost because they couldn't follow their maps.

For many years every explorer who tried to reach the North Pole died or turned back. Finally, on April 9, 1909, a team made it. This team was led by Robert E. Peary and his right-hand man—Matthew Henson. After almost twenty years of hardship, Henson, Peary, and four Inuit stood at the North Pole. They had crossed 10,000 miles of Arctic lands and seas to get there.

Why did these men succeed when others had failed? What made this team so successful? To answer these questions, it is necessary to understand Peary and Henson and the times in which they lived.

Henson and Peary were very different men; yet they came to depend on each other. Peary was ten years older and six inches taller than Henson. Peary was white, well educated, a naval officer, and an engineer. Henson was African American, an orphan, and self-educated. It is surprising that men so different would become a team.

When Henson and Peary met, the Civil War was over, but racism still kept people apart. In most of the country blacks and whites could not eat together, stay in the same hotels, or work in the same places. Things were changing in other ways, however. Explorers were traveling to places no one had been before and claiming lands for their countries. This opened doors for many people—black and white.

President Theodore Roosevelt was proof of these changing times. Roosevelt was an adventurer. A sickly child, he worked hard to strengthen his body and improve his health. As an adult, Roosevelt hunted wild animals in Africa, rode with cowboys, and climbed mountains. He saw life as a series of challenges to overcome. He wanted Americans to focus on challenges. One of these challenges was to claim new lands to achieve greatness and to unite the country with pride.

Roosevelt said, "I preach to you then, my countrymen, . . . If we shrink from the hard contests . . . then the bolder and stronger peoples will pass us by." He said that the country would become great by taking risks.

Reaching the North Pole was a worthy contest. Roosevelt wanted an American to claim the Pole. The race to reach the North Pole had started in 1871. Over the years explorers from many countries had tried and failed to reach the North Pole.

Peary wanted to raise the American flag at the North Pole. As a child, Peary had read about an explorer named Kane and his brave explorations. *Could Peary succeed where Kane had failed?

In 1886 Peary took a leave from the navy to explore the island of Greenland, which lies near the North Pole. On Greenland, Inuit villages crowded together in the stark white landscape. Inuit people had saved Kane when he had failed to reach the North Pole in the mid-1800s.

Peary went to Greenland because he wanted to see if a route from Greenland to the North Pole was possible. He decided it was. A year later, Peary met Henson in a store in Washington, D.C., where Henson was working. The two men began talking and found they had a lot in common.

Like Peary, Henson was no stranger to travel or the sea. An orphan, Henson left home when he was just 11. When he was 13, he went to sea as a cabin boy on a sailing ship. He loved the* ocean.

Henson was bright and willing to learn. At sea, the captain of the ship taught him many things he would have learned in school, such as math and history. Henson also learned how to navigate and how to chart a course as he traveled all over the world.

When the captain died, Henson returned to the United States. Henson had many skills, but he found it hard to find work because he was an African American. Finally he got a job as a store clerk.

While the two men were talking, Peary learned that Henson was determined and resourceful. Henson also was strong and skilled in many ways. Henson could build and fix things as well as navigate a ship.

Peary hired Henson to work with him in Nicaragua. That trip was the start of a partnership between the two men that lasted for 22 years.

In 1891 Henson joined Peary on his first trip to the Arctic. Peary had raised money for this trip and again had taken a leave from the navy. He took his wife and six others. But Henson was the most important member of the group. Henson built their houses and other equipment. His skills were exactly what Peary needed to reach the Pole.

In the Arctic, Henson was welcomed into the Inuit culture as if he had been born into it. Because of his skin color, the Inuit thought Henson was one of them. The Inuit taught Henson their language and about their culture. They taught him how to build an igloo, how to make clothing from a polar bear skin, how to find food in the Arctic region, and how to drive a dogsled.

Henson was one of the main reasons Peary's team survived. Henson was the only one who could handle the dogs, build and repair the equipment, including the dogsleds, and talk with the Inuit people. Peary needed Henson, and everyone knew it.

But this life was good for Henson as well. As an explorer and sailor, he had more freedom than he would have had in the United States. He was not treated badly as African Americans often were at home.

When the group returned to the United States, Peary wrote of Henson, "He is a better dog driver and can handle a [dogsled] better than any man living, except some of the best Inuit hunters. I couldn't get along without him."[1]

Henson and Peary went on a speaking tour to raise money for their next trip to the Arctic. Peary spoke about their experiences, and Henson drove the dogsled and spoke Inuit. They raised enough money to sail again in 1893.

There were many problems on this trip, and most of the team returned home early. Only Henson and another man, Hugh Lee, stayed with Peary. As they headed for the North Pole, one disaster after another struck. They were freezing and starving.

Peary and Henson hunted musk oxen for food. When one of the oxen charged Peary, Henson killed it with his last bullet. By the end of the trip, they had crossed almost 450 miles of ice cap. They took huge meteorites back to the United States. But they had failed to reach their goal—the North Pole. At the same time explorers from other countries had traveled to within 225 miles of the North Pole.

In 1898 Peary and Henson tried again. They were racing against another explorer who was trying to reach the North Pole. This time Peary got frostbite and had to have several toes removed. After that, he could walk only with a sliding step. When Peary had recovered from losing his toes, the team headed north again.

In early 1902 they left the ice cap, which covered land, and started out over the Arctic Ocean. The ocean was covered with ice that cracked and shifted under their feet. Henson led the way, but by April they came to a mile-wide channel of open water. These channels of water are called *leads.* The team could not move forward and had to turn back.

When they returned, President Roosevelt praised Peary's team for setting the American record for traveling closest to the North Pole. But they had made it to only 350 miles of the Pole. They had to try again. Peary worked on a new plan and a new ship.

The ship was named the *Roosevelt* in honor of the president. It was made to smash through the ice. The ship could ram ice floes and break them apart. Peary and Henson sailed north again in 1905. They took Inuit with them to set up base camps and to help them make a trail.

Henson and Peary were stopped again at the same mile-wide lead. They waited days for ice floes to jam so they could cross. Then they were caught in a snowstorm and ran out of food.

When they finally made it back to the ship, they found that, despite the ship's design, the ice had crushed the *Roosevelt.* The crew filled the holes in the ship as best they could and started home. Hurricanes pounded the ship, and the crew expected it to sink. Somehow they made it home by the end of 1906. They had not reached the North Pole, but they had set the world record for going farthest north.

The next year Henson married Lucy Ross and planned to settle down. Now that Peary was 50 years old and Henson was 40 years old, they had only one more chance to make it to the North Pole.

One reason Peary respected Henson was that Henson was the only person Peary knew who wanted to be "first" as much as he did. At the North Pole, nature tested all men, no matter what their race. On their last trip Peary and Henson would learn something they had not thought about before—only one person could be first.

Peary's and Henson's attempts to reach
the North Pole

Chapter 2

One Last Time

July 6, 1908

To the roar of the crowd in New York harbor, the *Roosevelt* set sail again, carrying Peary and his crew. President Roosevelt was on hand to cheer the men as they left. If anyone could win the race to the North Pole for the United States, it was Peary!

Peary was no ordinary man, and the *Roosevelt* was no ordinary ship. It had been rebuilt to withstand the ice. This time the pressure of the ice would not crush the *Roosevelt* if it became trapped in a frozen sea. Peary had big plans for the *Roosevelt.* The ship was going to take his group as far north as a ship had ever sailed. Then they would travel across the ice to the North Pole by dogsled, with teams setting up base camps along the way.

*Some people did not think Peary should take an African American man on the trip. But Henson knew that Peary needed him on the trip to the North Pole. Henson knew about sailing, and he knew how to build and repair necessary equipment.

Others on the team also knew that Henson was extremely valuable to the team's success. He was widely known as one of the best dogsled drivers in the world, he knew the Inuit language well, he was liked by the Inuit, he could build snow houses, and he made the sleds they would use on the route to the Pole.

The men had carefully planned every detail of their trip. They remembered their failed trip in 1906, when they had to turn back within a few hundred miles of the North Pole. Their food and water had nearly run out. If Henson had not killed a musk* oxen for them to eat, everyone would have starved. The crew had been bitterly disappointed.

Peary's skills were well known at the turn of the twentieth century. He had been in the navy for many years, and he had a background in engineering. The plan he came up with to reach the North Pole in 1908 had been carefully worked out. This time he left no detail of his trip to chance.

Peary's plan cost a lot of money. They had to bring much more with them on this trip than on earlier trips. Peary wanted to be sure that a lack of food and water would not keep them from reaching the North Pole again.

Peary and Henson did not make the trip in 1908 by themselves. There were five other men on board the *Roosevelt*—Robert Bartlett, who was captain of the *Roosevelt;* Dr. John Goodsell; Donald MacMillan, who was a math teacher; Ross Marvin, a professor of engineering; and George Borup, a young, educated sportsman.

August 1, 1908

When the *Roosevelt* reached Greenland in August, Inuit families greeted the team. They remembered Henson and called him by the Inuit name they gave him, which meant "the kind one."

Henson cared a great deal for the Inuit. "I have come to love these people," he wrote in his diary. "I know every man, woman, and child in their tribe."

Feeling right at home, Henson spent the next week trading with the Inuit for supplies and dogs. He got more than 200 strong, healthy sled dogs to take with them. They were important to the success of the trip. Only a few of those dogs would survive the trip and reach the North Pole.

Inuit sled dogs are part wolf and are used to being outdoors. They do not need shelter at night. Instead, they curl up in the freezing winds and sleep with their noses under their tails.

The leader of the pack is called the "king dog." He becomes the king dog by fighting the other dogs for their respect. The king dog is the one that keeps all the others in line on the trail.

At one Inuit village the men learned that another team, led by Dr. Frederick Cook, was also trying to reach the Pole. Cook had been a member of Peary's failed Arctic trip in 1891. Peary did not believe Cook was skilled enough to beat him to the Pole. Even so, Peary still felt he should hurry.

By August 18, the *Roosevelt* had the people, dogs, and supplies needed to start the next leg of the trip. On board were tons of whale and walrus meat, hunting equipment, and coal. Besides the seven explorers, there were about 40 Inuit and 250 dogs. Only the best Inuit sled drivers and hunters had come with Peary.

The ship set sail. As it moved, the temperature began to drop. The ship pushed its way through the packed ice, looking for flowing water. As soon as a route opened, it quickly closed again.

The *Roosevelt* frozen in

At one point the ship was closed tightly in jaws of ice, unable to move. Luckily, the ice shifted during the night. The *Roosevelt* was free once more. But for the next three weeks, the crew fought for every inch the ship moved forward.

Meanwhile, everyone on board was working hard. The Inuit women used animal skins to make warm clothing for the men. They chewed the skin for hours to make it soft enough to sew. The men made dog harnesses from walrus hides.

September 5, 1908—Ellesmere Island

Finally the ship reached northern Canada. The group stayed at Cape Sheridan in Canada until the spring thaw. The men built wooden houses on the shore. Peary had the best cabin. It had a private bathroom and bathtub. A picture of President Roosevelt hung on the wall, and there was even a piano in the room.

During the layover, Peary planned a new kind of sled to take them to the Pole. He wanted a sled that would carry heavier loads. He knew that attention to detail could mean the difference between success and failure—even life and death.

All winter Henson built the sleds Peary had designed. The runners were longer than those on other sleds. They curved up at the ends, so the sled looked like a canoe.

To make a sled, Henson and the crew used the Inuit way of lashing, or tying, pieces together. Nails and screws would not work in this bitterly cold place. Nails and screws made the sled too stiff; it could crack in half on the ice. Lashes helped the sled bend and twist as it moved over icy ridges.

The sun was sinking a little more each day. Soon the Arctic would be dark for six months. The men hurried to find enough food to last them through the winter.

The dogs had to stay behind while the men hunted. The dogs did not like to be left behind. They were tied in teams, and they started fighting with each other because they were bored. Henson was not surprised. He knew the dogs did better in times of hardship. When the dogs led an easy life, they would get sick and would often die. When they were without food in the harsh Arctic winter, however, they would pull the sleds and inspire the people to keep moving.

Peary had told the men that he could take only one person with him to the Pole. Henson had stuck with Peary through many other trips. Henson had helped Peary through many problems. But no one knew for sure that Peary would take Henson. What would his country think if Peary chose an African American over five white men for this honor?

February 1909

The winter sky in the Arctic was dark. Far to the south, a thin band of light appeared. It was the first hint of the sun's return. Every day there would be a little more sunlight. Peary wanted to beat the spring thaw. Cape Columbia would be the last stop before the dangerous journey across the frozen Arctic Ocean.

Timing is important in the Arctic. Between December and June the sunlight increases. At one point the sun shines 24 hours a day. Peary knew that the sun could be deadly in the Arctic because sun melts the ice. Those who cross the thawing ice risk death. A person could fall into frozen water or become trapped under ice. No one can live for long in such icy water.

Terrible Arctic storms delayed Peary and Henson's trip. Arctic winds can pick up 150-pound rocks and throw them 100 feet. Even Peary was not safe from these storms.

In 1894 a storm had picked up a 100-pound box of supplies. The box had hit Peary, putting him out of action for a week.

Peary knew he could wait no longer. He wanted to start the race to the Pole. To reach the Pole, the team needed enough daylight to see and ice frozen strongly enough to support their weight. If they waited any longer, the trip would be more dangerous because the ice would start to thaw.

The team put on their new clothing— reindeer suits and polar-bear-skin pants. New sealskin boots kept their feet warm. Peary knew from experience how important good boots were, after losing toes to frostbite in 1898. However, this loss did not stop him from making the race to the Pole. He had learned to slide his boots instead of walking.

Chapter 3

Heading for Cape Columbia

February 18

Peary gave the signal, and the men set out. The men broke into teams. Captain Bartlett led the first team to Cape Columbia. Dr. Goodsell's team left the following day. A few days later, Henson's team left. Each sled was loaded with enough food to feed the men and the dogs as well as metal cooking stoves, fuel to heat the stoves, and furs.

Over the next few days, the weather was so cold that the thermometers did not work. The men built walls of snow to protect their campfires from the wind. The team tried to move forward, but it was too cold. Ootah, an Inuit hunter and the most respected member of the tribe, suffered from frostbite. The team stopped at a nearby camp so he could rest.

When they set out again, the sleds sank into the soft, melting snow. In order to keep moving, Henson and his team had to pick up the sleds and carry them, trying hard not to spill any of the supplies. Henson's will was like steel. He told the men they had to move forward no matter what. They had started toward the Pole, and Henson would not turn back.

February 22—Cape Columbia

At last they reached Cape Columbia. Henson spotted the igloos of the first two teams before he saw Captain Bartlett or Dr. Goodsell. Cape Columbia was going to be their base camp.

The dark Arctic days and nights were slowly draining the men's spirits. The men were starting to feel dark and moody, just like the landscape. Dr. Goodsell did not look well. Henson feared his friend was getting sick.

When Captain Bartlett returned from hunting, he looked tired and frustrated. Even worse, he had been unable to kill anything for them to eat. Bartlett was so hungry that Henson gave Bartlett all of his dinner. Peary's team and Marvin's team were due to arrive, so there was no time for the explorers to rest. Henson started moving supplies to different base camps along the trail. The plan was for the parties to act like relay teams. Each of the five teams would take turns going ahead to set up a camp for the other teams. When a team arrived at the next camp, igloos and supplies would be waiting for them.

February 24

It was 45 degrees below zero. The wind whipped into the igloos. It even blew away Dr. Goodsell's igloo. Henson helped him build another one.

There was no way for the explorers to get away from the cold. The snow was blinding. The men were stuck inside, so they passed the time by reading. Each man had brought along a favorite book to read. It was a rare time of rest for the explorers.

*For a while, they forgot the danger.

But soon the sun began shining longer each day. The men noticed the light growing in the distance. By March the sun turned bright red, and the sky was blue and wild. The clouds were light and round. In one way this was helpful to Henson and the other men. The shadows, sun, stars, and moon have always been an explorer's tools. Henson knew how to navigate by the stars. Now Marvin taught him how to navigate by the sun.

Henson went outside to take the temperature reading. It was 57 degrees below zero. Henson had seen it lower, but he once said that after 40 below the difference was too small to be noticed.

Henson looked to the north. There was the ice-covered ocean. They had to work their way through its dangers. Henson saw another danger sign—dark, heavy clouds.* He knew that the clouds meant there was open water ahead. But the men couldn't think too much about the dangers or they might lose their will to go on.

Peary arrived at the camp in a hurry. He did not want to stop. He began giving orders right away, telling the men what they needed to do. Bartlett and Borup loaded their sleds, left Cape Columbia, and pushed forward onto the ice of the Arctic Ocean.

February 28

A new leg of the trip had begun. They were only 413 miles from the North Pole!

Peary wrote in his diary: "We are ready now for the final lap of the journey. . . . It is the time for which I have reserved all my energies. . . ."

Over the next few days, teams moved the supplies of food, the fuel, and the dogs to a group of base camps across the ice. The sleds were piled high. Each dog needed a pound of food each day to keep going. Fifty dogs needed 500 pounds of food every ten days. That's why supply camps along the trail were so important.

The men had all the navigational tools they needed to help them figure their location. Flags, including the American flag, were neatly folded on Peary's sled. They would be used only once—when the explorers had reached the North Pole. The men had also brought cameras to record the event.

One flag had been with Peary on every Arctic trip he had made. On each trip Peary cut a small strip of cloth from the flag and left it at his "farthest north" point. No one else ever saw those "flags" because the ice shifted and they were lost.

Soon Peary would begin sending teams back to the ship to get more food. Before leaving the *Roosevelt,* Peary had told

MacMillan that Henson must go all the way with Peary. Peary said he could not make the trip to the North Pole without Henson. But Henson did not know this at the time.

March 1

In his diary Henson wrote, "We were all excitement and at attention. A strong wind was blowing, which we took as a good [sign]. . . . We were ready . . . awaiting the command, 'Forward! March!'"

Henson cracked his whip, and the dogs were off, yelping with happiness. They had been waiting for the chance to run. At first the young ice was smooth. But then the trail became rough, and Henson's sled split. He had to use his bare hands to sew it back together.

It takes patience, control, and will to repair a sled in the frozen Arctic air. Each day Henson had to build new sleds from broken ones. Even if other groups passed him, he could not rush the job.

In his diary Henson wrote about fixing the sleds. ". . . with ungloved hands, thread the sealskin thongs through the hole. The fingers freeze. Stop work, pull the hand through the sleeve, and . . . put your hand under your armpit, and when you feel it burning, you know it has thawed out."

Henson fell behind the other teams, and soon he found himself in last place. But being in last place made the ride easier for his team. The other teams had already cut the trail, and Henson's sled could follow in their tracks.

Battling hardships, the teams continued. The wind was so cold and strong that the men could see their breath freeze on the fur of their hoods.

It was too cold.

The men built igloos. In the Arctic climate, igloos are better than tents. Igloos are warm and airtight and will not let in snow or water. Peary knew that igloos did not have to be taken down and carried on the sled but could be left behind to be used on the return trip. Peary wanted his men to be able to build a strong igloo in only 45 minutes. Henson was the only one who could do it.

The men spread out their furs for beds, but it was too cold to sleep. During the night Henson awakened over and over again because of the cold. He beat his arms and feet to keep his blood moving. Otherwise, they would have frozen.

Remember the goal.

They had to remember the goal. Although they were hungry and tired, they set out again the next morning.

The snow had become too soft and deep for the sleds. Even though they used the wide snowshoes, the men would sink to their knees in the snow. The dogs were buried up to their chests. The sleds often turned over.

After covering only seven miles, the men stopped by open water. Leads, or channels of water, were everywhere. It was a sign of what was to come.

Henson decided that crossing the lead on a block of ice was too risky. He tried to walk around the flowing water, but he could not.

By the next day a patch of new, solid ice had formed. But the explorers did not trust the new ice. They feared it might break under the weight of the teams and the sleds. But Henson took the chance, and they crossed the lead on the new ice.

Two miles later they reached an island of ice. They stopped to mend the sleds and to wait for the other teams to catch up. Soon all the teams had caught up except Borup's team. Marvin was sent to look for them.

Suddenly the ice began to shatter around the men. The sound was earsplitting. The men pushed forward and somehow managed to get out of danger.

That was their last brush with danger for a while. During the days that followed, the men enjoyed ideal conditions on the ice. Henson called it the best traveling on sea ice he had experienced in 18 years. The dogs were able to run, and that helped the teams make up for lost time. Henson did not stop to sleep at the first camp. He decided to keep going, even though Borup and Marvin had not returned.

March 7

The men approached what they thought was the longest split in the ice. Henson thought it had to be the same lead that had given them trouble three years before. To cross this lead, the men had to wait for it to freeze over.

The conditions that spring caused many of the men to get frostbite. The frozen sea was thawing, but the temperature of the air was still below freezing. If the men got even a small amount of water on their skin, it could turn to ice. After the ice was removed, the skin could not heal. MacMillan got frostbite while they were waiting for the lead to freeze over. His heel kept freezing. Then his boots stuck to his skin, which could not heal.

Several days passed. They watched the lead but could do nothing but wait. Bartlett grew silent. Goodsell read and wrote in his diary. In spite of the frostbite, MacMillan told jokes and played games with the other men. But Peary was in a hurry to move on.

Slowly ice began to form, and the lead froze over. But then Peary changed his mind and decided to wait for Marvin and Borup. More days passed. Two of the Inuit wanted to go back to the ship. Angrily, Peary sent them back.

Had they waited too long and missed the chance to cross?

Chapter 4

One False Step

March 11

The day was clear. The temperature read 45 degrees below zero. The lead had finally frozen, but it was not completely solid. It was still dangerous to cross. In spite of this, the men finally heard Peary say, "Off we go!"

For the time being, the greatest danger was over. However, they had lost many days of good weather waiting for Borup and Marvin, who still had not caught up.

Speed was very important at that point. Too many men and dogs would slow the pace. Every detail was important. The men decided that the weakest people and animals would return to the ship.

Henson told Peary that MacMillan was not fit to continue and that some Inuit should go back.

March 14

MacMillan and Goodsell, along with the Inuit men and some of the dogs, were sent back to the ship. Inuit then brought a message that Marvin and Borup had safely crossed the lead and would soon reach the rest of the teams.

The group moved on. Henson led the next five marches, hoping to make good time. But the weather was extremely cold—49 degrees below zero.

Also the snow was deep and too soft. The dogs knew the conditions were rough, and they did not want to go on. First they became stubborn and would not move. Then they grew wild with fear. They did not listen when Henson and the others gave orders to them. When they finally moved, the dogs sank beneath the soft snow. The sleds also sank with the dogs. Henson and the others had to dig the dogs from the snow pits and carry them across the ice.

The dogs also had to be carried over each pressure ridge, which is an ice wall that forms when the wind freezes ocean waves. Pressure ridges can be 20 to 50 feet high and are one of the hardest things to cross. The men had to cross some each day. They made footholds in the ice with picks. It took two men to push one sled over a pressure ridge onto more level ice. Sometimes the men had to unload the sleds, carry the supplies over, and repack the sleds on the other side.

Henson wrote in his diary: "I was as tired out as I have ever been. I was carrying the full-loaded [sleds] with about 550 pounds, while the other parties in the lead never carried but half of the regular load."

Heading across the ice to the North Pole

March 16

Ootah, the most experienced Inuit, took the lead. One false step by anyone could mean death. Ootah led them safely across in single file. But they were not out of danger. Three sleds broke, and the explorers were forced to camp while Henson and the others made two sleds from the remains of three broken ones. As they finished, Peary, Bartlett, Borup, Marvin, and their teams arrived.

March 18

There were more broken sleds to fix. The air was thick with haze and frost. Heavy winds pushed at the men's backs. According to Henson, "The wind would find the tiniest opening in our clothing and [stick] us like needles."

The men did not feed the dogs. Experience had taught them that sled dogs worked better with the hope of food as a reward.

As the men continued, day after day, they wondered how far north they were. Marvin checked their location. He recorded the angle of the sun, which would tell him what time it was. By knowing the time, he could figure out the latitude, or distance north or south of the equator.

March 19

*The new ice was smooth and easy to travel over, but crossing it was dangerous. Strong wills kept the men going.

Henson and his men forced the dogs to run across the sleek ice as quickly as they could. The dogs raced across the ice with their tails tucked against their bodies. They barked and yelped over and over again. Suddenly the ice cracked open, and one sled fell into the water. The Inuit driver escaped, but the load with Henson's extra equipment and clothing was soaked. But the dogs managed to drag the sled to safety.

Then another disaster struck. One sled fell 30 feet, and its load spilled down the ice ridge. The dogs tried to get away from the sled. They panicked because they were still attached to the broken sled. They became tangled in their harnesses.

Henson rushed over and calmed the dogs with kind words* and pats on the head. Peary caught up to them and saw what was happening, but he said nothing. That night, however, he called Henson to his igloo.

He told Henson that they would continue, but some of the men and weaker dogs had to go back to the ship. Henson was not surprised. He had known that only a few men would last the entire trip to the Pole.

— Chapter 5—

Only Two Teams

March 20

*The sun was now shining 24 hours a day. There was no darkness.

That night Peary talked with Borup. Peary told Borup that his team would not make it to the Pole. The next morning Borup led the third party back to the base camp.

The return trip would be faster for Borup and the others. Those going back to the ship would follow the trail left by the other dog teams. The camps along the way were already set up and stocked with food and supplies. The men hoped the good weather would hold. If a storm hit, they might die on the ice.

Two groups were left. The men decided that Bartlett, Henson, and their teams would go ahead and make the trail.

Peary, Marvin, and their teams would sleep while the first teams made the trail. Then Peary and Marvin would travel over the fresh trail while* the other teams slept.

March 21

Henson woke to find that Bartlett had already left. Henson knew that nothing counted as much as speed at this point. He hurried to catch up with Bartlett.

March 22

A perfect day for travel greeted Henson and his team. The ice was clear and smooth for miles. There was no wind. The sky was blue. The good weather raised their spirits. They hoped the weather would last.

March 23

How quickly things changed! The men had to carve their way through the ice, inch by inch. Henson and Bartlett turned over their igloos to Marvin's party and began the next leg of the trip.

March 25

Henson awakened at 4:30 A.M. to a snowstorm. Peary told the men that they had to speed up. He told Henson that another group of men had to be sent back to the ship. Henson still did not know if Peary wanted him to go all the way to the Pole. He was worried that his team would be sent back.

But soon Henson learned that Marvin was to be sent back to the ship. Marvin had frostbite on his feet, and his skin was turning black. Henson relaxed. There was only one person left between him and the Pole. That person was Captain Bartlett.

March 27

Once again Henson chose the best dogs and sorted the loads. He visited Marvin's igloo to say good-bye to his friend.

Marvin never made it back to the ship. After Henson returned from the North Pole, he learned that his friend had died.

The Inuit claimed that Marvin had fallen through the ice and drowned. However, the truth was that Marvin threatened one of the Inuit. The Inuit shot him and buried him in the ice.

March 29

The men were tired, hungry, and thirsty. There was snow everywhere, but they could not eat the snow to quench their thirst. If they did, their body temperatures would become too low. They had to wait until they reached camp. There they could boil water to drink.

By that night they had traveled farther north than any other known humans. The entire group was together, and everyone was in good shape. Still, Peary had said that one more group would be sent back to the ship. During the night, a loud roar suddenly awakened them. The ice floor of their igloos was breaking up!

Everywhere they looked, pieces of ice were breaking off and spinning in the water. The men feared for their lives. Still half asleep, the men grabbed the terrified dogs and dashed across the ice to safety.

Everyone made it except Bartlett. His igloo had separated from the others. He was trapped on an ice floe that was spinning across the water. But then the ice floe bumped into a larger ice floe, and Bartlett and his dogs safely crossed.

April 1

The day came when the last team was to be sent back to the ship. Peary knew that the only man who could help him get to the Pole was Henson. Peary told Bartlett that he must return to the ship. Bartlett accepted the news, but he was not happy. He bid his friends farewell and bravely wished them good luck. They watched him leave on the 300-mile trail back to the *Roosevelt*.

Henson wrote in his diary, "Commander Peary and I were alone the same as we had been so often in the past years, and as we looked at each other, we realized that the time had come for us to demonstrate that we were the men who should unlock the door which held the mystery of the Arctic."

Without wasting another second, the two men pushed off across the smooth ice. They were in the final race!

Matthew Henson

Robert E. Peary

Chapter 6

At the Top of the World

*Henson wanted to go to the Pole as much as Peary did. The men were together, but they were also competing in the race to the Pole. There are many different versions of this part of the story. But the version in this book is Henson's story and that of the Inuit who were with him.

Henson understood that Peary would get the credit for finding the Pole. They were all part of the same team, but Peary was the leader. Peary noted in his diary that he had stayed in the background to help men who were having trouble and to fix problems: ". . . From here on, I shall take my proper place in the lead. . . ." He did not stay in front all the time, but he did take the lead.

Close to the Pole the ice is smooth because the ocean is very deep. There are few ridges, unlike* the ice over shallower water. But the ice was beginning to melt. Peary and Henson traveled 25 miles at a rate of 1.5 miles per hour. They pushed on before the midnight sun melted the ice.

Once again Peary was afraid of failing to reach the North Pole. He did not care about sleep. They charged ahead. They would fall and get up, but they would not stop. It was as if the wind and the sun were pushing them forward.

Henson knew they were getting close to the Pole. He studied the stars, the sun, and the ice to determine their latitude.

April 3

Henson crossed the moving ice, pushing his sled across. That sled had all the tools needed to measure distance. Suddenly his feet began to slide. The sled slipped from him toward a hole in the ice.

Henson crashed into the frozen water of the Arctic Ocean. He feared it was the end of his trip and perhaps the end of his life. He knew he could freeze to death.

Henson struggled until " . . . old Ootah grabbed me by the nape of the neck, the same as he would have grabbed a dog, and with one hand he pulled me out of the water, and with the other hurried the team across. He had saved my life, but I did not tell him so, for such occurrences are taken as part of the day's work. . . ."

Ootah saved the sled and the tools as well. Henson was soaking wet. He took off his sealskin boots and beat the water from his pants. He put on dry boots and hurried to catch up to the others. He learned that Peary had also fallen into the water.

April 4

The team took a short rest and then returned to the trail just before midnight. Peary ran ahead to lead the dogs. One sled ran over his foot, but he barely felt it. Only one thing was on his mind—he hoped for three more days of good weather. That was how long he thought it would take to reach the North Pole.

April 5

The North Pole is at exactly 90 degrees latitude. Peary was sure they had reached 89 degrees. The ice was smooth, and they had made good time. But Peary described the cold as being like frozen steel.

April 6

Henson was in the lead. He traveled by foot with the Inuit. The men had covered a great distance. Henson decided to stop— and for good reason. He wrote in his diary, after calculating how far he'd gone, that either he was on the Pole or he had already passed it.

Henson told the Inuit to make an igloo. The dogs settled themselves into balls of fur and rested.

Peary was 45 minutes behind Henson on the trail. When he arrived, he asked Henson how many miles they had gone. Henson told him that he thought they were sitting on the Pole. He later wrote in his diary of that moment that Peary got extremely mad, even though he didn't say anything.

Peary took many readings with the navigational tools that measure distance and location. The bright snow and sunlight hurt Peary's eyes as he was taking the readings. It would be several days before his eyes returned to normal. Henson took down the readings as Peary called them out. Finally Peary seemed content that they had reached the Pole.

Henson stepped up to Peary. "I ungloved my right hand and went forward to congratulate him on the success of our 18 years of effort."

Peary did not shake Henson's hand, and Henson decided that Peary had not seen it.

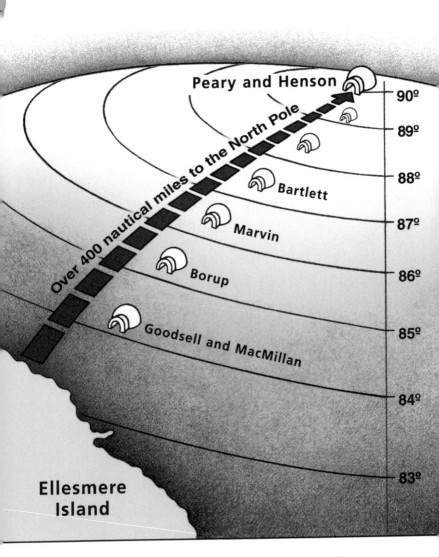

Peary used teams in relays to reach
the North Pole.

Peary pulled out the old flag. He told Henson, "This . . . is to be . . . the last and most northerly camp on the earth."

He planted the flag on top of the igloo. Cheers rang out across the frozen sea.

The men took more readings and took many pictures. One of them shows Henson and the four Inuit holding flags.

Using a telescope, they looked in all directions for nearby land. But they did not see any land. All they saw was ice. There was no land to claim for the United States. They had reached just a point on a map.

Peary and Henson tried to measure the ocean depth. They lowered a weight into the water, but after lowering it 9,000 feet, they had still not found the bottom.

The men remained at the Pole for 33 hours. Then they began the trip back to the *Roosevelt.* They had to travel over 400 miles of dangerous, icy trails. They knew the spring thaw might strand them on the ice forever, so they moved quickly, sleeping only a few hours each day. On April 23—just 17 days later—they arrived at the ship. Henson described the return trip as "17 days of haste, toil, and misery as cannot be comprehended by the mind."

Peary did not speak to Henson more than a few times during the entire trip back. Henson was unsure why this was so, but it saddened him. Was Peary angry because he had to share the glory? Was it because he was not the first? Henson thought of all that he and Peary had been through together. His heart was heavy.

When they reached the ship, the men rested for several weeks. They needed to regain their strength. It was July before the ice broke up enough for the ship to set sail for home.

October 2—New York City

When the *Roosevelt* docked in New York City on October 2, a cheering crowd was there to greet the explorers.

Americans were full of pride. Reporters talked to Peary, but Henson was ignored. Peary told the story of how he raced ahead those last hundred miles and became the first man to stand at the North Pole. A few lines in the newspaper talked about Peary's "colored servant," but no one used Henson's name.

Five months later Dr. Cook claimed that he had reached the Pole a year before Peary. When Congress investigated Peary's claim, Henson was not called as a witness. At that time, many white Americans did not believe what an African American man had to say. But Cook's lie was uncovered, and Peary was given the highest honor given to an explorer—the Hubbard Medal from the National Geographic Society. Henson was ignored once again. The second highest award was given to Bartlett, who had not even reached the Pole.

Peary retired from the navy with a pension. Henson was out of work. He asked Peary to help him, but Peary refused. Henson said later, "For the crime of being present when the Pole was reached, he has ignored me ever since."

In 1920 Henson read in the newspaper about Peary's death. Friends said Henson got up and went into the bathroom. He turned on the water, perhaps so they could not hear him weeping.

Peary was given a hero's burial in Arlington National Cemetery. On his headstone are the words "ROBERT EDWIN PEARY, DISCOVERER OF THE NORTH POLE."

Nearly 30 years after Peary and Henson reached the North Pole, Henson was given some credit for his part. In 1937 he became the first African American in the Explorer's Club, of which Peary had been president. In 1944 Congress awarded a medal to all who had gone on the trip, including Henson. He visited the president in the White House.

Henson died on March 9, 1955. He had a simple burial. In 1988 his grave was moved to Arlington National Cemetery alongside Peary's. Then he, too, was given the hero's burial he deserved.

To the Inuit people, Henson had always been a true hero. Years after the trip, Ootah said that he would always tell how Henson made it to the Pole.

Does a place or a dot on a map remember? In Greenland, stories can survive for a long time. There the story of Henson and the North Pole reaches higher than the trees—higher even than the mountains. It is moved along by the cracking sound of blocks of the ice floes, the rush of the wind, and the blast of Arctic storms. In that place, at the top of the world, the story of Matthew Henson and the race to the North Pole will live forever.